THE ILLUMINATED ALPHABET

BY
THEODORE MENTEN

DOVER PUBLICATIONS, INC., MINEOLA, NEW YORK

Copyright © 1971 by Dover Publications, Inc.
ISBN-13: 978-0-486-22745-0
ISBN-10: 0-486-22745-6

Manufactured in the United States by Courier Corporation
22745623
www.doverpublications.com

E

F

12

F

H

K

L

M

Q

34

R

U

U

V

V

X

X

Y

48

Z